Today's children have around 6000 new titles published especially for them in the English language each year. This adds up to a much greater range of books from which to choose than at any other time in history. But what is even more impressive than the large *quantity* of books available is the very high *quality* of these books. They are, in general, superbly written, illustrated, edited, designed and produced.

In addition, access to books has never been easier. Cost need not prevent children from enjoying good reading, since the work of the best authors is available in inexpensive paperback editions and through book clubs. Many children are also well served by school and public libraries.

This book offers a graphic and attractive introduction to some of the stories written by 15 of the world's best and most popular children's authors. Their distinctions are many: most of them have won coveted awards, such as the Carnegie Medal (UK) and the Newbery Medal (USA). Some, such as Margaret Mahy, Katherine Paterson and Jan Mark, are multiple winners of these prizes.

Though all but one of these authors come from the United Kingdom or the United States, they are well known in countries around the world, through translations of their work into other languages — proof that children's literature, at its best and most imaginative, can be a powerful link between different peoples and cultures. For children's literature is largely about universal matters — happiness and joy, fears and concerns, hopes and aspirations, relationships, love and faith. It offers young people everywhere reassurance that they are not alone, that their problems are not unique but are universal and solvable, and that while there may be evil and injustice in the world, honesty, goodness and justice *can* prevail.

Books can give children a sense of their own worth and of their place in the world. But most of all they feed the imagination, giving the spirit wings to soar.

Acknowledgements

The author and publishers are grateful to the following for permission to reproduce copyright material:

Joan Aiken: Penguin Books and Pan Piccolo for covers; Rod Delroy for photo. Lucy M. Boston: Penguin Books for covers. Judy Blume: Pan Piccolo for covers; Charles Bush (Pan Books, London) for photo with son; Thomas Victor for photo. John Christopher: Penguin Books for covers and photos. Beverly Cleary: Puffin (Penguin Books), Morrow, Hamish Hamilton, Scholastic Book Services and Julia MacRae (Franklin Watts) for covers; Sandra Hansen (W. Morrow & Co.) for photo. Nina Bawden: Puffin (Penguin Books) for covers; Nina Bawden for photo. Roald Dahl: Cape Books and Penguin Books for covers; Penguin Books for photos. Alan Garner: Armada Lion and Collins Books for covers. Mollie Hunter: Pan Piccolo for covers. Ursula Le Guin: Penguin Books and Gollancz for covers, maps and decorations; Lisa Kroeber (Gollancz) for photo. Margaret Mahy: Dent for covers; Christchurch Press Co. for portrait; Auckland *Star* for photos. Jan Mark: Penguin Books for covers and photos. Katherine Paterson: Crowell and Puffin Books (Penguin) for covers; Jill Paton Walsh (Penguin) for photo. Cynthia Voigt: Fontana Lions, Atheneum and Collins for covers; Walter Voigt for profile; U.S. Travel and Tourism Administration for photo of Annapolis Harbour.

The author would like to thank Pat Adam (Penguin Books, Australia) for her assistance in making available illustrative material for this project.

First published 1989 by
THE MACMILLAN COMPANY OF AUSTRALIA PTY LTD
107 Moray Street, South Melbourne 3205
6 Clarke Street, Crows Nest 2065

Associated companies and representatives
throughout the world

McVitty, Walter, 1934—
   International children's authors.

   Bibliography.
   ISBN 0 333 47787 1.

   1. Children's literature — Bio-bibliography. 2. Authors — Biography.
   I. Title. (Series: Australian colour library).

809'.89282

Set in Helvetica by
Savage Type Pty Ltd, Brisbane
Printed in Hong Kong

The Australian Colour Library

International Children's Authors

Text by

Walter McVitty

Contents

M

△ Joan Aiken, one of the most original and imaginative of children's writers, was born in Rye, Sussex, England, on 4 September 1924. She comes from a literary family: her father was Conrad Aiken, the well-known American poet; her sister Jane Aiken Hodge is also a writer. Joan Aiken was educated at home by her Canadian-born mother until she was 12 years old; she then went to Wychwood, a boarding school at Oxford (1936–40). After leaving school she worked in a variety of jobs, first for the British Broadcasting Corporation (1942–43), then as a librarian in the United Nations Information Centre in London (1943–49). She was a sub-editor and features editor for *Argosy* magazine (1955–60), and an advertising copywriter for J. Walter Thompson, London (1960–61). She began writing full-time in 1962 and has since had more than 40 books published, for adults as well as children. In addition to her novels, she has also published collections of original short stories, plays and poetry, as well as retellings and translations. She has won many prizes for her work, including the *Guardian* Award (1969) and the Mystery Writers of America Edgar Allan Poe Award (1972).

She says of her work: 'I alternate between writing for adults and writing for children so as to use a different set of muscles. When writing for children a simpler vocabulary produces a simpler plot line. It also creates more straightforward characterisation, a direct flow of time sequence, no flashbacks, few internal communings or complicated moral issues. Otherwise the process is identical.'

▷ Joan Aiken has written a group of books which have been called 'unhistorical fiction' because they all take place during a period of British history which never existed! For these books she supposed that there was a Stuart King, James III, who came to the throne in 1832 and remained there, in spite of the plotting of supporters of a 'Hanoverian pretender'. During the reign of James III, Joan Aiken imagined the north of England as a place where wolves roamed wild, hence **The Wolves of Willoughby Chase** (1962), one of her most popular novels of this period. Conspiracies to dethrone good King James III are the subject of **Black Hearts in Battersea** (1964) and **Night Birds on Nantucket** (1966) in which rebels plan to assass... the King by means of a lo... cannon fired across t... Nantucket in Ameri... Palace in London. ...ca to ...James... **Cuckoo Tree** (1971), ...the ti... been succeeded ... James III... **Stolen Lake** (198... Richard IV. **The** America, where peasset in Roman... Latin and the legendary... Art... still lives, with a fat and sinist... 1300-year-old Guinevere. The young heroine of these novels is a resourceful, sharp-eyed Cockney waif named Dido Twite, whose self-confident manner, daring escapes and colourful language have made her a favourite with readers.

THE SHADOW GUESTS
Joan Aiken

GO SADDLE THE SEA
Joan Aiken

THE WHISPERING MOUNTAIN
Joan Aiken

◁ Joan Aiken is a leading writer of short stories, which are often found in general anthologies as well as in books of her own collections. Some of the collections are for younger children, such as: **A Necklace of Raindrops** (1968), **The Kingdom Under the Sea** (1971), and **Fog Hounds, Wind Cat, Sea Mice**. Others such as: **A Bundle of Nerves** (1976), **All You've Ever Wanted** (1953), and **More Than You Bargained For** (1955), are for older children. The stories in these books are sometimes modern fairy-tales and sometimes fantasies about talking, or at least extra-intelligent, animals.

Married to Julius Goldstein, an American professor of art, Joan Aiken spends half of each year living in an apartment in New York, U.S.A., and the other half at 'The Hermitage', her large home in Petworth, West Sussex, England. When not writing, she particularly enjoys gardening.

◁ Joan Aiken is a superbly skilled writer of dramatic novels of adventure, excitement and suspense. **The Shadow Guests** (1980) is a realistic story set in the present, with elements of the past and the supernatural. **Go Saddle the Sea** (1977) is an adventure story set in Spain in the early 19th century. **The Whispering Mountain** (1968), which won the 1969 *Guardian* Award, is the story of a stolen Welsh bardic harp, a wicked Marquess and a lost tribe of dwarfs who live inside a whispering mountain.

▽ Nina Bawden's earliest children's books were conventional adventure stories, usually involving secret passages, people being trapped in caves, kidnappings, and the evil deeds of jewel thieves and other crooks who are outwitted in the end and brought to justice by clever children. A change in her writing towards greater realism occurred in **Squib** (1971). In **Squib** some children encounter a badly neglected and mistreated boy and learn that the realities of life can be 'more frightening than a hundred old witches'. Nina Bawden is especially interested in crime and criminals, and the workings of justice as, apart from being a writer, she is also a Magistrate for the County of Surrey.

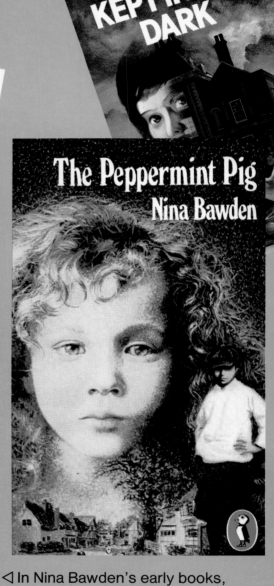

◁ In Nina Bawden's early books, children always outwitted crooks and had them brought to justice, but in **The Robbers** (1979), two boys who begin by acting out their fantasies about thieves find themselves in very serious danger. Like most of her work from **Squib** onwards, **The Robbers** is more true-to-life than earlier works. It is set on the banks of a canal in Islington, the inner-London suburb where the author now lives.

◁ During World War II, along with thousands of other London schoolchildren, Nina Bawden and her young brother were evacuated from London to the safety of a small mining town in South Wales. One of her best books, **Carrie's War** (1973), is based on her experiences during this time. In the book, Carrie and her young brother Nick have to learn to cope with the peculiar people with whom they are billeted; Samuel Evans, a bitter, rigid, narrow-minded, bullying shopkeeper, and his kindly but downtrodden sister, Lou. Carrie reappears years later, married to Albert Sandwich whom she met in **Carrie's War**, in **Rebel on a Rock** (1978), a political thriller set in a country resembling Greece. In **Rebel on a Rock**, Carrie's children become involved in a conspiracy to free the country from a dictatorship.

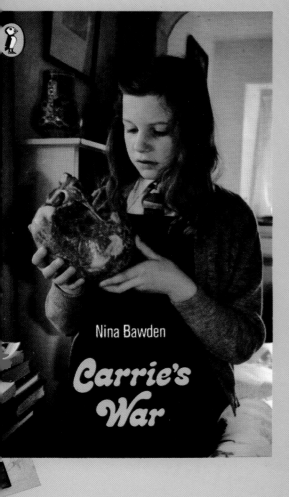

△ English author Nina Bawden was born in London on 19 January 1925. She was educated at Ilford County High School and Somerville College, Oxford, where she obtained a B.A. degree (1946) and an M.A. (1951). Nina Bawden began writing when she was very young, and wrote her first novel when she was eight years old: 'I wrote plays for my toy theatre and an epic poem in blank verse about a beautiful orphan with curly golden hair — my own was straight and black!' She began writing novels for adults in 1953 and only thought of writing for young readers when her own children asked her to write a story about an exciting adventure they had had:

'It took me just as long as writing an adult book. But I enjoyed writing it so much that I thought I would like to write some more. I find that I enjoy it more than writing adult novels. The things I write about for adults I write about for children too: emotions, motives, the difficulties of being honest with oneself, the gulf between what people say and what they mean. When I write for children I am writing from the point of view of the child who still lurks inside me, still hopeful, still trusting, who sees the world as a place that is potentially full of exciting adventure and who likes to tell, and be told, a good tale about it.'

Nina Bawden finds that writing for adults sometimes provides ideas for children's books. For instance, **Kept in the Dark**, a psychological thriller for children, is a reworking of ideas from **Devil by the Sea**, a book written for adults.

◁ **The Peppermint Pig**, which won the 1975 *Guardian* Award, is based on the childhood of Nina Bawden's mother in Norfolk at the turn of the century. Johnnie the Pig — a household pet — actually existed: 'A little pig, sitting in a pint beer mug and squealing.'

Here is the opening passage from this enjoyable book:

Old Granny Greengrass had her finger chopped off in the butcher's when she was buying a leg of lamb. She had pointed to the place where she wanted the joint to be cut but then she decided she needed a bigger piece and pointed again. Unfortunately, Mr Grummett, the butcher, was already bringing his sharp chopper down . . .

'What happened afterwards? Did she spout blood?'

'No, it was a clean cut,' mother said . . .

Poll said suddenly: 'If he sold it to eat, I expect it would taste like a sausage with bone in it.'

'More meaty,' Theo said. 'They put bread in sausages.'

▽ Popular American author Judy Blume was born on 12 February 1938 in Elizabeth, New Jersey, where most of her books, including **Are You There, God? It's Me, Margaret** (1970), are set. She obtained her B.A. degree from New York University, married in 1959 and settled in Westfield, New Jersey, where she had two children, a daughter, Randy, and a son, Larry. After a divorce she re-married in 1976 and went to live in New Mexico, the setting for **Tiger Eyes** (1981).

Judy Blume wrote her first book for children in weekly instalments, as a student exercise for a course in creative writing. 'Writing about young people comes naturally to me because I am blessed with almost total recall. Young people ask me how I know their secrets. It's because I remember just about everything from age eight on, and many things that happened before that. I write sometimes from my own experiences, sometimes from my children's, and other times by imagining how I would feel and react if placed in a certain situation. I'm not sure where my ideas come from. I'm just grateful that when I finish one book there is usually a new idea waiting for me. I let each book evolve naturally. I find the first draft pure torture. Once that's finished I can relax, for it is the rewriting process that I really enjoy.'

▷ An author's own children often provide good ideas for books, through the things they do and say. Judy Blume's son, Larry, now grown up, shown here with his mother, was the model for the character Judy Blume called Fudge in **Tales of a Fourth Grade Nothing** (1972) and **Superfudge** (1980). Nothing is safe around Fudge (real name Farley) unless it is nailed to the floor! He enjoys plastering his baby sister's head with stamps — and hiding her in secret places! Judy Blume says, 'Like Fudge, my son Larry really did spread mashed potatoes on the wall of a restaurant.'

Judy Blume receives lots of fan mail from young readers all around the world. She says, 'I'm really thankful for the thousands of letters I receive from my young fans each year. I owe my career to my readers!' Her popularity is due to the realistic way in which she portrays the lives and problems of young people growing up. She is able to do this convincingly because she draws on memories of real things that happened in her own childhood in New Jersey and her own thoughts and feelings at that time. In **Otherwise Known as Sheila the Great** (1972), the things that bother Sheila (such as a fear of lightning) bothered Judy Blume when she was that age. **Starring Sally J. Freedman as herself** (1977) is her most autobiographical book: 'When I was ten I was a lot like Sally, making up stories inside my head.' Judy Blume's most popular book is **Are You There God? It's Me, Margaret** (1970). 'Margaret is myself, when I was in Sixth Grade. Her thoughts, concerns and feelings were my own.' Eleven year old Margaret is anxious about growing up, the changes which will come with puberty, and the decisions she will have to make about her own life: 'How can I stop worrying,' she asks, 'when I don't know if I'm going to turn out normal?'

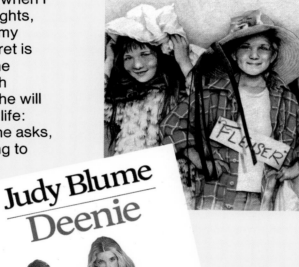

The Judy Blume Diary; the place to put your own feelings (1982) was published to encourage children to record their own thoughts and experiences, just as Margaret does in **Are You There God? It's Me, Margaret**: 'Sometimes just writing down your feelings makes them easier to understand. Even if you are lucky enough to have someone with whom you can discuss anything, there are still times when you don't want to share your thoughts . . .'

◁ Not all of Judy Blume's books are based on her own childhood experiences. 'Ideas seem to come from everywhere,' she says. **Blubber** (1974), a story about a girl who is treated badly by everyone else at school because she is fat, came from an incident that took place in Judy Blume's daughter's classroom. **Deenie** (1973) is the story of a girl who suffers from scoliosis, curvature of the spine, a disability ignored by her mother, who has plans for her to be a model. The idea for this story came from meeting, at a party, a woman who refused to recognise the limitations of this handicap in her own daughter. Judy Blume wrote **It's Not the End of the World** (1972), about a family break-up, after her own divorce: 'I wrote it because I knew many families who were suffering the pains of divorce. Perhaps my book would help them come to terms with it.' **Tales of a Fourth Grade Nothing** (1972) came from reading a newspaper report about a child who had actually swallowed a pet turtle!

◁ July Blume divides her time between New York City and the mountains of New Mexico. **Tiger Eyes** is set in New Mexico. It is about a fifteen year old girl and her family. Judy Blume says: 'It's my first book set in New Mexico, where the scenery is so beautiful I sometimes have to face the wall in order to write.'

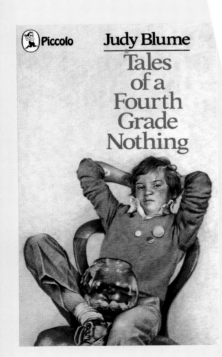

△ Lucy (Maria) Boston was born in Southport, Lancashire, England, in 1892. She was educated as a boarder at Downs School, Seaford, Sussex, then at a finishing school in Paris, before going to Somerville College, Oxford (in 1914). She cut short her university education to train in the Voluntary Aid Detachment, St. Thomas' Hospital, London, and served as a nurse in France during World War I. In 1917 she married an English officer and had one son, Peter (who illustrated her children's books).

▷ The Green Knowe series of books is based on Lucy M. Boston's house. **The Children of Green Knowe** (1954) introduces a house and its owner, Mrs Oldknow, who tells her great-grandson Tolly stories of the children who lived there in past centuries. Tolly meets these children in this book and its sequel, **The Chimneys of Green Knowe** (1958). **The Stones of Green Knowe** (1976) tells how the house was built in the 12th century. In **A Stranger at Green Knowe** (1961) Hanno, a gorilla who has escaped from the London Zoo, seeks refuge in a bamboo thicket at Green Knowe. The real bamboo thicket, in Lucy Boston's sunken hedge garden at Hemingford Grey, can be seen in the photograph at the bottom of the next page.

Not every Lucy M. Boston book is about Green Knowe. **The Sea Egg** (1967) is a fantasy set on a Cornish beach. Lucy Boston writes that: 'It is almost wholly an evocation of sense perception. The sound of the sea is on every page.'

▽ As well as being an outstanding writer, Lucy M. Boston is also a gifted linguist, musician and painter. Her Austrian landscape, shown below, dates from the early 1930s, when she was studying art in Vienna. After World War I Lucy M. Boston lived on the continent. She returned to England to live before the outbreak of World War II. She did not begin to write for publication until she was 60 years old, and won the 1962 Carnegie Medal for her fourth book, **A Stranger at Green Knowe** (1961).

The River at Green Knowe

Lucy M. Boston

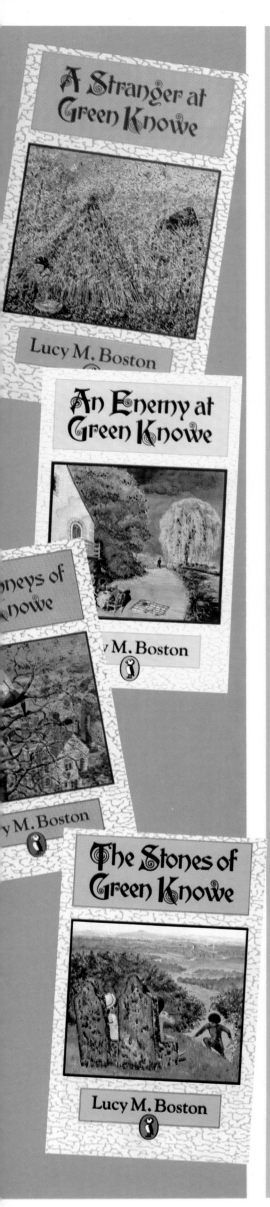

A Stranger at Green Knowe

Lucy M. Boston

An Enemy at Green Knowe

y M. Boston

[n]neys of [n]nowe

y M. Boston

The Stones of Green Knowe

Lucy M. Boston

▽ ▷ In 1939, after many years in Europe, Lucy Boston returned to England and was lucky enough to be able to buy this 700-year-old manor house, in the village of Hemingford Grey, Huntingdonshire, not far from Cambridge. The manor house, which is said to be the oldest inhabited house in England, fronts onto the River Ouse, which was described in **The River at Green Knowe** (1959). The house was once surrounded by a moat for protection, in the days when the river was navigable from the sea. When Lucy Boston bought the house, it had been 'renovated' but, with the help of her son Peter, she began uncovering and restoring its original Norman interior, and researching its history. She regards the house as being 'alive', and full of the continued presence of those who have lived in it over the centuries. This ancient house, with its powerful atmosphere of the past is in fact, the major 'character' in the Green Knowe books. She says of it: 'I have found the place I need and this is where I stay, getting deeper in it every moment and always surprised. A lifetime could be spent researching into it. But I just sit and talk to it. I live in it alone and find it good company.' In **The Chimneys of Green Knowe**, one of the characters, Tolly, says: 'I like this house. It's like living in a book that keeps coming true.'

▷ A lover of gardening, Lucy Boston is shown here beside the topiary work on her front lawn.

Betsy Byars was born in Charlotte, North Carolina, USA, on 7 August 1928. She spent her childhood in Charlotte and remembers: 'I was a happy, busy child. I started sewing when I was very young because my father worked for a cotton mill and we got free cloth. I was making my own clothes by the second grade. I could make a gathered skirt in fifteen minutes. I sewed fast, without patterns, and with great hope and determination, and that is approximately the same way that I write.

'When I was young, I was mainly interested in having as much fun as possible. Adults were always saying to me, "If only you would take your piano lessons (or Math or English) seriously." Enjoying things was just more important to me than taking things seriously.'

▽ As an adult, Betsy Byars still enjoys herself. She and her husband Ed both have pilot's licences and are keen on flying and gliding: 'This means putting the plane together, taking it apart, holding a fifty-pound wing tip over my head for long periods of time, polishing the wings and taping the joints. Gliding makes up a big part of our spring and summer activities.'

◁ Betsy Byars won the Newbery Medal 'for the most distinguished contribution to American literature for children' with **The Summer of the Swans**, but her first critical success was **The Midnight Fox** (1968). When Betsy Byars wrote **The Midnight Fox** 'We were living in West Virginia and we had a cabin up in the mountains. I had seen a fox. It was really something special for me. That sparked a book. It was the first book in which I had used my own children. I used a lot of personal things they were doing and things from my own childhood. It seemed to work.' That approach has worked successfully ever since.

▷ Betsy Byars is surprised that she became a writer: 'At school I had absolutely no interest in writing. I liked the outdoor life. However, I could already read quite well when I started school but I thought then that writers must have the most boring life in the world, sitting and typing all day by themselves. Now that's what I do, but I have never been bored.'

△ Betsy Byars was educated at Furman University in South Carolina and then at Queens College, Charlotte. After graduating she married Edward Ford Byars, a professor at Clemson University, in 1950. She now lives in Clemson, South Carolina, with her husband and children (three daughters and one son). She began writing magazine articles in 1956 and, as her children grew, she became interested in writing books for young readers. She says of her writing: 'My books begin with something that really happened, a newspaper story or an event from my children's lives. But, aside from this mutual starting point, each book has been a different writing experience . . . It takes me about a year to write a book, but I spend another year thinking about it and polishing it.'

Betsy Byars usually writes realistic stories about believable children and teenagers attempting to find solutions to genuine problems in their daily lives. She has a simple, direct style and is very skilful in presenting and developing characters and issues: 'The story has to take place in a very short time — one, two or three days — I want the story to take place quickly. I like to take ordinary people and throw them in a crisis.'

▷ John Christopher, England's leading science fiction writer for children, was born in Knowsley, Lancashire, in 1922. He was educated at Peter Symonds' School in Winchester, a city which features in many of his books. He first worked in a local government office and served in the Army Signal Corps during World War II. After the war he worked in the information bureau of a diamond cutting firm and began writing novels and magazine stories for adults in his spare time, producing up to four books a year. Financial success enabled him to move to Guernsey, in the Channel Islands, where he continued to write, full-time, for 20 years, before returning to Rye, Sussex, where he now lives. Twice married, he has four daughters and one son, from his first marriage. He has won many prizes for his writing, including the *Guardian* Award and the Rockefeller-Atlantic Award.

◁ Using pseudonyms such as Anthony Rye, William Godfrey and Peter Nichols, as well as his own name, John Christopher had written fourteen novels for adults before his publisher Hamish Hamilton asked him to try writing science fiction for young readers. The result was **The White Mountains** (1967) and its sequels **The City of Gold and Lead** (1967) and **The Pool of Fire** (1968). These books make up the 'Tripods Trilogy'. Set in the future, when Earth is dominated by oppressors from a distant planet, the books tell how three boys join with rebels in their struggle against the alien Masters and their Tripod machines.

▷ In **Fireball** (1981) two boys, Brad and Simon, are torn from this world through a blazing ball of light and transplanted into a parallel time in which present-day Britain is still occupied by ancient Romans. After a Christian revolution, the boys escape to a wood cabin in Canada. In a sequel, **New Found Land** (1983), they are snowed in and surrounded by hostile Indians. Their only hope for survival is to travel south by raft across the freezing waters of the North Atlantic. In **Dragon Dance** the boys are captured by Chinese slavers and taken from California to China. These three books make up the 'Fireball Trilogy'.

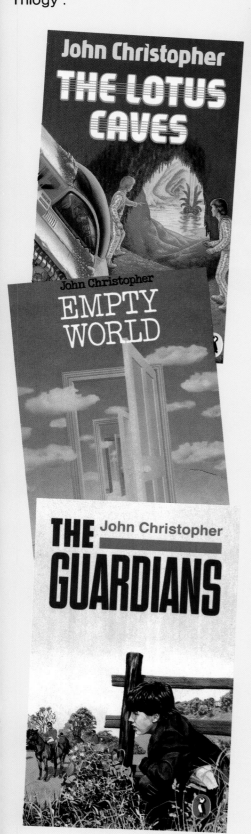

◁ **The Lotus Caves** (1969), **Empty World** (1977) and **The Guardians** (1970) are separate books and not parts of a trilogy. In **The Lotus Caves** two boys, Mark and Steve, bored with their dull, safe life in a huge, sterile bubble on the moon, steal a 'crawler' and go joyriding beyond the legal limits. When the 'crawler' falls through the moon's crust, the boys find themselves in an eerie and dangerous land below. In **Empty World**, a virulent plague is sweeping across the world, killing off adults, leaving the world to young people — and, finally, to Neil Miller. The book is the story of his battle for survival against both the plague and his fear and loneliness. In **The Guardians**, winner of the 1971 *Guardian* Award for children's literature, young Rob Randall escapes from a grim and merciless city of the not-too-distant future and experiences life in the idyllic countryside; where he thinks he is safe!

△ The 'Prince in Waiting Trilogy' consists of three books **The Prince in Waiting** (1970), **Beyond the Burning Lands** (1971), and **The Sword of the Spirits** (1972), which tell of life in a future England which has been devastated by volcanoes and earthquakes and divided into warring city-states. Luke is the Prince in Waiting, heir of the ruler of one of the settlements dotted all over England after the Great Disaster. He has been chosen by the Seers to be the hero who will re-unite his country. In the end, Luke, acclaimed as Prince of Winchester, loses his bride, his friends and the city he had inherited.

△ Popular American writer Beverly Cleary was born, an only child, in McMinnville, Oregon, on 12 April 1916. She spent her early childhood on a farm. She went to school in Portland, Oregon before attending Chaffee Junior College, Ontario, California, and finally the University of California at Berkeley, from which she graduated with a B.A. degree in English. She then entered the School of Librarianship at the University of Washington, in Seattle, to specialise in library work for children. She was a children's librarian at Yakima, Washington, until 1940, when she married and went to live in Oakland, California. During World War II she worked as a military hospital librarian at Oakland. She now lives at Carmel, California, which is close to the sea. She has twin children, a boy and a girl.

In 1975 Beverly Cleary won the Laura Ingalls Wilder Award for her 'substantial and lasting contribution to literature for children'. In 1984 she won the John Newbery Medal which was awarded for 'an outstanding contribution to American literature for children' to her book **Dear Mr Henshaw**.

She says of her work: 'As a child I had difficulty learning to read. The discovery, when I was about eight years old, that I could actually read, and read with pleasure, was one of the most exciting moments of my life. From that moment on, as I read through the shelves of the library, I searched for, but was unable to find, the books I wanted to read most of all: books about the sort of children who lived in my neighbourhood, books that would make me laugh. The stories I write are the stories I wanted to read as a child, and the experience I hope to share with children is the discovery that reading is one of the pleasures of life and not just something one must do in school.'

◁ **Fifteen** was a forerunner of the modern 'young adult problem novel'. Although originally published in 1956, this story of a girl's first romance, her self doubts and anxieties about growing up, is still popular today. Other teenage novels by Beverly Cleary are **Jean and Johnny** (1959), **The Luckiest Girl** (1958) and **Sister of the Bride** (1963). Although these books might seem romantic and dated now (drugs, alcohol and sex play no part in them), they contain believable characters finding their way through adolescence. The slow processes of self-discovery and the formulation of personal values which the books show, are matters of relevance in any generation.

◁▷ 'Unless you count an essay I wrote when I was ten years old (I won two dollars, because no one else attempted the contest), **Henry Huggins** was my first attempt at writing for children.' **Henry Huggins** (1950), was about the adventures and problems of an eight year old boy, his dog Ribsy, and his friends, the troublesome Ramona and her older sister Beezus. They all live on Klickitat Street in the city of Portland, Oregon, where the author spent her own childhood. Henry Huggins is a healthy, normal boy who is constantly involved in comical situations. Henry Huggins was an instant success with readers. The story led to many more books about Henry, Ramona and Beezus, each of whom grows a little older with each new book.

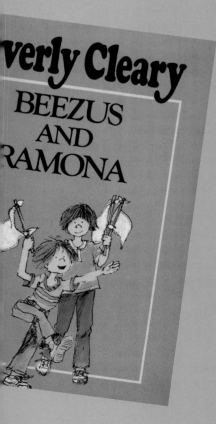

△ As well as writing realistic stories about everyday, ordinary children, Beverly Cleary also writes fantasy stories, such as **The Mouse and the Motorcycle** (1965) and **Runaway Ralph** (1970). Ralph is a motel mouse who rides a toy motorcycle given to him by one of the guests, a young boy who is able to talk with him. Beverly Cleary says, 'This book came about after several years of wondering how I could write a book about motorcycles that eight-year-old boys would enjoy. One day the thought crossed my mind that a mouse was just the right size to ride the miniature motorcycle my son owned. That was the beginning of the book.'

Beverly Cleary won the 1984 John Newbery Medal for **Dear Mr Henshaw**, the story of a lonely boy who writes letters to the author of a book called *Ways to Amuse a Dog*.

Roald Dahl is one of the world's most popular authors of children's books. He was born in Llandaff, Wales, on 13 September 1916, of Norwegian parents. Believing an English education to be superior to all others, they sent him to Repton School, Yorkshire. Roald Dahl wrote unfavourably about his bizarre schooldays at Repton in **Boy** (1984), the first part of his autobiography.

At the age of 18 Roald Dahl went to Africa to work for the Shell Oil Company and was there when World War II began. He has written about this period, and his subsequent adventures as an RAF fighter pilot, in **Going Solo** (1986). 'I joined a fighter squadron in the western desert of Libya in 1940 and was promptly shot down by the Italians. I spent six months in a hospital in Alexandria and rejoined my squadron in Greece flying Hurricanes. When the Germans kicked us out of Greece, we flew against the Vichy French in Syria. Then my old injuries caught up with me, and I was invalided home to England. In 1942 I was sent to Washington, D.C., as an Assistant Air Attache and that was when I started writing.' Chris Powling has written a profile of Roald Dahl especially for children.

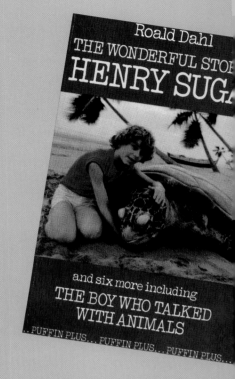

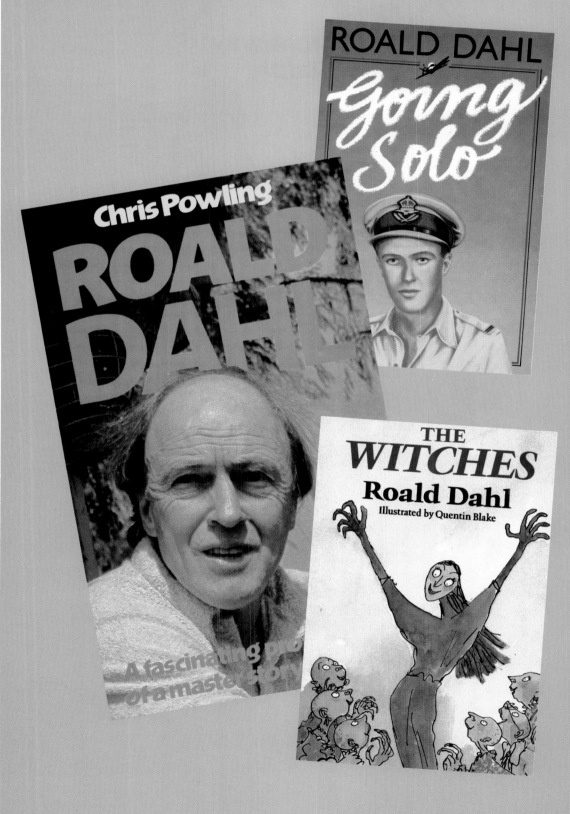

▷ Roald Dahl keeps a notebook in which he jots down ideas for stories: 'Just about every children's book I have ever written has started out as a three or four line note in this little, much-worn red-covered volume.' For example the note 'What about a chocolate factory that makes fantastic and marvellous things — with a crazy man running it?' became **Charlie and the Chocolate Factory**. Another note: 'A man acquires the ability to see through playing cards. He makes millions at casinos', was the basis for the novel **Henry Sugar**. **Fantastic Mr Fox** began as: 'A story about Mr Fox, who has a whole network of underground tunnels leading to all the shops in the village. At night he goes up through the floorboards and helps himself.' The note for **The Boy Who Talked With Animals** was: 'A boy pleads with his father to buy a captured turtle and release it.'

Roald Dahl says, 'I spent at least twenty years of my life writing nothing but short stories for adults, but then our first child came along. When she was old enough to have stories told to her at bedtime, I made a point of making up a story every single night. It became a routine that continued when our second child came along. Had I not had children of my own, I would never have written books for children, nor would I have been capable of doing so.'

◁ Roald Dahl has a special talent for macabre humour — and this extends to the writing of comic verse. **Revolting Rhymes** is a retelling, in verse, of six well-known nursery tales — with surprising twists:

As soon as Wolf began to feel
That he would like a decent meal,
He went and knocked on
  Grandma's door.
When Grandma opened it, she
  saw
The sharp white teeth, the horrid
  grin,
And Wolfie said, 'May I come in?'
Poor Grandmamma was terrified,
'He's going to eat me up!' she
  cried.
And she was absolutely right.
He ate her up in one big bite.
But Grandmamma was small and
  tough,
And Wolfie wailed, 'That's not
  enough!
I haven't yet begun to feel
That I have had a decent meal!'

△ Roald Dahl writes his books in a hut in the back garden of 'Gipsy House', his residence in Great Missenden, Buckinghamshire. He works to a set routine, writing from 10 a.m. to 12.30 p.m. and from 4 to 6 p.m. each day, always sitting in the old armchair above. His 'desk' is a plywood board which rests on a roll of corrugated paper. In cold weather he keeps his legs warm by placing them in a sleeping bag which is pulled up to his waist!

▷ Alan Garner won the 1967 Carnegie Medal for his novel **The Owl Service** (1967), a modern-day story based on an old Welsh myth, and inspired by the pattern on the dinner plate shown here. Alan Garner's stories begin when, 'An isolated idea presents itself. It can come from anywhere. Something that happens; something seen; something said. I react to it, usually forget it; but it is filed away by the subconscious. Later, another idea happens involuntarily, and a spark flies. The two ideas stand out clearly, and I know they will be a book.' For **The Owl Service** Alan Garner says, 'I first read the Welsh myth of Lleu Llaw Gyffes and the wife who was made for him out of flowers, who destroyed him and was herself turned into an owl. Then I happened to see a dinner service that was decorated with an abstract floral pattern. The owner had toyed with the pattern, and had found that by tracing it, and by moving the components around so that they fitted one another, the model of an owl could be made. It was then that the spark flew.'

▷ Alan Garner spends much time, sometimes years, researching material for his books. Cadellin, the wizard in his first children's books, **The Weirdstone of Brisingamen** (1960) and **The Moon of Gomrath** (1963), is a character in the local legends of the people who live in or near Alderley Edge, Cheshire, where the Garner family has lived for generations. **Elidor** (1965) is based partly on the ballad of Childe Rowland:

'Before writing **Elidor**, I had to read textbooks on physics, Celtic symbolism, unicorns, medieval watermarks, megalithic archeology; study the writings of Jung; brush up my Plato; visit Avebury, Silbury and Coventry Cathedral; spend a lot of time with demolition gangs on slum clearance sites; and listen to the whole of Britten's *War Requiem* nearly every day.'

▷ A major theme in the life and work of Alan Garner is the influence of the past on the present, the 'timelessness' of life and events. In **Red Shift** (1973), small groups of people from three different periods in English history — Roman Britain, the Civil War and the present — undergo similar experiences. The events are interwoven, to give the impression that 'it is all happening at once'. The book is based on the ballad of Tam Lin (or Tamlain). As the text is mainly dialogue, the result is a puzzle which the reader has to work out. 'I reveal the kind of book it's going to be at the start. If you don't like what you read in the first few pages, nothing's going to get any better. I write in such a way that whoever reads it has to engage their own responses creatively in order to get the potential out of the book. My stories are never explained.'

◁▽ As well as writing stories Alan Garner has compiled and written a number of collections of myths, legends, fairy tales and folklore.

▽ Alan Garner was born in Congleton, Cheshire, England, in 1934. He was educated at Alderley Edge Primary School, Manchester Grammar School and Magdalen College, Oxford, where he studied languages and linguistics. He served in the Royal Artillery as a Second Lieutenant before starting a full-time career as a writer, not just of children's books but also of plays for radio and television, and poetry. He likens his books to onions: 'A book must be written for all levels of experience. This means that any given piece of text must work at simple plot level, so that the reader feels compelled to turn the page, if only to find out what happens next. My concern for the reader is not to bore him. An onion can be peeled down through its layers, but it is always, at every layer, an onion, whole in itself. I try to write onions.'

▽ Alan Garner lives with his wife Griselda Greaves and their two children in 'Toad Hall', a mediaeval half-timbered brick farmhouse in Cheshire, close to the Joddrell Bank radio telescope. He saved the sixteenth-century apothecary's medicine-house on the right from demolition and had it rebuilt beside his fourteenth-century house, to which it is now connected. Romans once camped where the house now stands, and ancient Britons before them: 'When I began to write it was as important to me that I should find the *place* in which to work as it was that I should find something to write about. I found this house, and knew that here was where I must spend the rest of my life. I was not looking for escape. I was looking for a quietness in which to grow and take risks.'

Alan Garner is descended from a long line of Cheshire craftsmen — carpenters, wrightsmiths and stonemasons. In **The Stone Book** (1976) he imagines a few events in the lives of four succeeding generations of his own family, through finely written English — his own form of craftsmanship: 'I learned more technically about writing from a stonemason and carpenter who worked on my house, than from any other source.'

▽ ▷ Mollie Hunter's books fall into three categories — fantasy for younger readers (**The Kelpie's Pearls, The Enchanted Whistle, A Stranger Came Ashore**), historical novels for readers of twelve and over (**The Ghosts of Glencoe, The Lothian Run, A Pistol in Greenyards**) and realistic, part-autobiographical novels for young adults (**A Sound of Chariots, The Dragonfly Years**). She says that 'All three types of books, in effect, are simply varying facets of what I conceive to be the proper function of any writer, i.e. to entertain, and in the course of this to express something of one's own philosophy. To attempt this for young readers, I find, is a discipline as rewarding as it is exacting.'

△ Mollie (Maureen) Hunter is Scotland's most famous writer of children's books. She was born in Longniddry, East Lothian, on 30 June 1922 and educated at Preston Lodge School. She married in 1940 and has two sons. Her first book, **Patrick Kentigan Keenan**, was published in 1963. Since then she has written more than twenty books. She lives in a cottage called 'The Shieling' (a Scottish word for a shepherd's hut) in the village of Milton, close to Loch Ness. She says that, 'The child that was myself was born with a little talent, and I have worked hard, hard, hard to shape it. Yet even this could not have made me a writer, for there is no book can tell anything worth saying unless life has first said it to the writer. A philosophy has to be hammered out, a mind shaped, a spirit tempered. This is true for all of the craft. Talent is not enough — there *must* be a person behind the book.'

▽ Mollie Hunter's work reflects her deep love of Scotland — its landscape, people and history. 'I work for children because I like them as *people*, because I'm primarily a storyteller, and because the kind of tales I can spin for them are those that seem naturally to be suggested by a lifelong exploration of my own country's folklore and history.'

▽ ▷ In ancient times the inhabitants of the west coast of Scotland built circular, bottle-shaped stone towers, possibly as fortresses against Roman raiders searching for slaves. The ruins of some of these towers, called 'brochs', may be seen today in isolated valleys on the mainland, such as this one which is one of a pair at Glenelg, and on islands such as Skye and Lewis. Because these strange towers are found nowhere else in the world, and are identical in design and construction, Mollie Hunter believes that the idea of building the brochs must have come from one man, who travelled the coast supervising the building of them. **The Stronghold**, a story she wrote about an imaginary Orkney tribesman who might have been the architect of these brochs, won the 1975 Carnegie Medal.

▷ Ursula Le Guin is best known for her 'Earthsea trilogy' (**A Wizard of Earthsea** (1967), **The Tombs of Atuan** (1969) and **The Farthest Shore** (1972)), one of the most outstanding examples of modern-day 'high fantasy' writing. Like J.R.R. Tolkien's Middle-Earth stories, or the Narnia stories of C.S. Lewis, in Earthsea Ursula Le Guin has created an extremely vivid, imagined world complete with its own geography, dragons, customs, rituals, magic and language (Old Speech). Each book deals with dangerous quests, and the struggles between the forces of dark and light (good and evil) through the heroic and courageous wizard Ged, destined to be the most famous Mage of Earthsea. Born in a mountain village on the island of Gont, Ged serves an apprenticeship, using the name Sparrowhawk, at the great school for wizards at Roke. Tempted by pride to try spells beyond his powers, he lets loose an evil shadow-spirit in his land. Only he can destroy it.

△ Ursula Le Guin has also written novels for young adults. **A Very Long Way From Anywhere Else** (1976) deals with a romantic friendship between Natalie and Owen, two talented and unusual teenagers. This is a realistic story, set in today's world, but in **Threshold** (1980) Ursula Le Guin mixes realism and fantasy. Hugh and Irena meet in Tembreabrezi, a town in a magic world across the stream from the everyday world in which they have grown up. There they find peace and escape; until their refuge becomes horror, and they must choose between life and death.

◁ Illustrations from **A Wizard of Earthsea**.

△ Ursula Le Guin was born in Berkeley, California, U.S.A., in 1929, the daughter of an anthropologist and a writer. She was educated at Radcliffe College and Columbia University. She studied in France on a Fulbright Grant and married historian Charles Le Guin in Paris in 1953. She later taught French at universities in the United States. She now lives in Portland, Oregon, and has two daughters and one son. As well as writing fantasies for children and novels for teenagers, she writes poetry, short stories and science fiction for adults. Her main aim is to encourage the imaginations of children: 'One of the most deeply human, and humane, faculties we possess is the power of imagination; so that it is our pleasant duty, as librarians, or teachers, or parents, or writers, or simply grown-ups, to encourage the faculty of imagination in our children, to encourage it to grow freely, to flourish like the green bay tree, by giving it the best, absolutely the best and purest, nourishment that it can absorb. And never, under any circumstances, to squelch it, or sneer at it, or imply that it is childish, or unmanly, or untrue.'

△ Margaret Mahy is one of the world's most original, imaginative and skilful children's writers. Born at Whakatane, near the Bay of Plenty, on the North Island of New Zealand, on 21 March 1936, she went to school in Whakatane and to universities in Auckland and then Christchurch, where she qualified in librarianship. For many years she was a children's librarian at Canterbury Public Library, but she now works full-time as a writer. She lives at Lyttelton, on the South Island of New Zealand, in a house she partly built herself which overlooks the sea and is close to Christchurch.

She says, 'I had an eccentric childhood. I believed I could understand what the birds and animals were saying (which alarmed my parents of course, although I don't remember them trying to change my behaviour). I ate grass and leaves, and insisted that other children accepted my fantasies. So I didn't have many friends. I've got quite a few now, having learnt that you can't force your imaginings on people.'

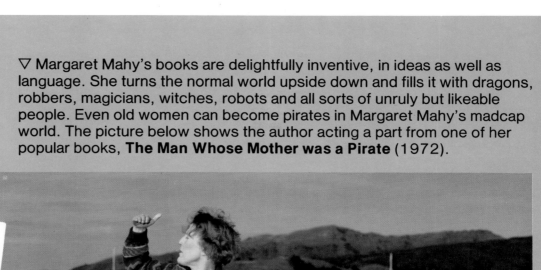

▽ Margaret Mahy's books are delightfully inventive, in ideas as well as language. She turns the normal world upside down and fills it with dragons, robbers, magicians, witches, robots and all sorts of unruly but likeable people. Even old women can become pirates in Margaret Mahy's madcap world. The picture below shows the author acting a part from one of her popular books, **The Man Whose Mother was a Pirate** (1972).

◁ ▷ Margaret Mahy began writing stories when she was seven and, since 1968, she has had more than fifty books published. As well as writing novels, she also writes picture-book texts, such as **A Lion in the Meadow** (1969), **Jam** (1985), **The Wind Between the Stars** (1976) and short story collections, such as **The Downhill Crocodile Whizz** and **Mahy Magic**. Margaret Mahy started to write for older children when her two daughters became teenagers. **The Haunting** (1982), **The Catalogue of the Universe** (1985), and **The Tricksters** (1986) were all Carnegie medal winners. These award winners and **The Changeover** (1984) are supernatural thrillers which are also stories about love, romance and family life. They are just as original and unusual as her stories for younger children. 'People tend to think of children's authors as people who are not very good at anything else. They don't realise the tremendous personal fulfilment in being able to do what you have deliberately chosen. Writing is like falling in love.'

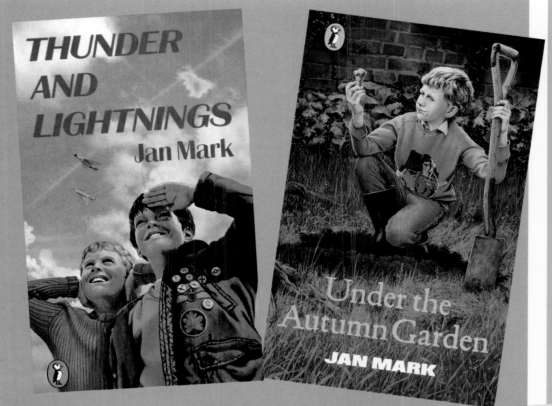

◁ Jan Mark won a Carnegie Medal with her very first book **Thunder and Lightnings** (1976). This book tells the story of the relationship between two boys, one of whom is a keen observer of the old Lightning fighter planes based at a nearby airfield. Her second book **Under the Autumn Garden** (1977) is about a boy who digs up his garden hoping to uncover the remains of an old priory for a school local-history project. The theme of both books, which are set in Norfolk, is the nature of friendship and change: 'Everything go. Everything go that you like best. That never come back,' says Victor, in his Norfolk English, in **Thunder and Lightnings**.

▽ Jan Mark was born in Welwyn, Hertfordshire, England, in 1943. She was educated at Ashford Grammar School, Kent (1954–61) and Canterbury College of Art (1961–65). She was a teacher at Southfields School in Kent (1965–71) before becoming a full-time writer. She is married with one daughter and one son, and lives in Oxford. She writes *about* children, but not deliberately *for* children: 'Since I do not know my audience in advance, I cannot aim at it. I can only try to write as well as I am able and hope to find a sympathetic response in anyone, of any age, who reads what I have written. I write to meet the demands of myself as an adult, not those of the child I once was.'

▷ Most of Jan Mark's stories are about relationships. In **Trouble Half-Way** (1985) Amy and her truck-driver stepfather get to know each other better on a trip to the north of England to see a cotton mill which has Amy's name written on it in huge letters. In **At the Sign of the Dog and Rocket** teenage Lilian has to run her parents' pub with the help of her school's young student-teacher, whom she dislikes. Erica, in **Handles** (which won the 1983 Carnegie Medal) loves motor-bikes and becomes friendly with the owner of a repair shop, whom she also likes! Stuck miles from anywhere, with her boring aunt and uncle, Erica discovers, 'the smallest industrial estate in the world' where she can indulge her love of motor-bikes among a bunch of characters with the unlikely 'handles' of Elsie (L.C. Wainwright), Bunny and the Gremlin. Erica longs to be accepted by them, and to have a handle of her own.

◁ Jan Mark is a versatile author who also writes: picture-book texts, **Out of the Oven**; easy-to-read stories for young readers, **The Dead Letter Box**; humorous stories, **Hairs in the Palm of the Hand**; stories about teenagers, **Frankie's Hat**; superbly crafted short story collections, **Feet** and **Nothing to be Afraid Of**; and quite difficult novels for mature readers, which are set on other worlds and are symbolic rather than naturalistic, **The Ennead, Divide and Rule**, and **Aquarius**. **The Ennead** takes place on Erato, a bleak planet on which all behaviour is rigidly controlled by the authorities.

▽ For many years Jan Mark lived in the Norfolk village of Ingham, close to the sea, and most of her books are set in this part of England, with its flat, fertile landscape which is dotted with farms, villages, windmills, and an extensive network of interconnected navigable waterways, called Broads.

▽ Katherine Paterson was born in Tsing-Tsiang Pu, China, on 31 October 1932. She went to the United States when she was eight. The daughter of missionary parents, she attended thirteen schools before graduating from Kings College in Bristol, Tennessee. She later obtained an M.A. in English Bible and spent the next four years in Kobe, Japan (1957–60), learning the Japanese language and assisting in church educational programmes on Shikoku Island. On her return to the United States she studied at the Union Theological Seminary in New York and met and married John Barstow Paterson, a Presbyterian minister. They live at Takoma Park, Maryland, with their four children, two of whom are adopted.

Katherine Paterson's first piece of writing was published in Shanghai when she was seven. Her first children's books **The Sign of the Chrysanthemum** (1973), **Of Nightingales that Weep** (1974), and **The Master Puppeteer** (1975) are all set in 12th Century feudal Japan. **Rebels of the Heavenly Kingdom** is set in China in 1850, at a time when the country was in a state of unrest and rebellion. It tells the story of Wang Lee, a peasant boy, who becomes a courageous warrior in a rebel army which is trying to overthrow the Manchu Emperor.

◁ As a response to the death of her youngest son's closest friend, Katherine Paterson turned from writing about life in Japan long ago to writing about American life today. The resulting book **Bridge to Terabithia** (1977), is a very moving story of the friendship between Jess, a country boy, and Leslie, a girl from the city. Together they share a secret place, Terabithia, which is an island in a dry creek bed. This outstanding book won the Newbery Medal.

▽ Gilly Hopkins, the heroine of **The Great Gilly Hopkins** (1978), is tough, cool and super intelligent and won't be had by anyone — teacher, social worker or foster parent. All she wants is to be reunited with her beautiful, long-lost real mother. Katherine Paterson wrote **The Great Gilly Hopkins**, which won the National Book Award in the U.S., as a result of her experience when she acted as an emergency foster parent.

◁ Katherine Paterson says about her work: 'My aim as a writer is to engage young readers in the life of a story that came out of me, but which is not mine but ours. I don't just want my readers' time or attention, I want their lives. I want their senses, imagination, intellect, emotions, and all the experiences they have known breathing life into the words upon the page. I hope to do my part so well that young readers will delight to join me as co-authors.

'The wonderful thing about being a writer is that it gives you readers — readers who bring their own stories to the story you have written, people who have the power to take your mythic, unbelievable, ten-foot-high characters and fit them to the shape of their own lives.'

Katherine Paterson

JACOB HAVE I LOVED

The memorable story of twin sisters — one loved, one hated — growing into womanhood

PUFFIN PLUS... PUFFIN PLUS... PUFFIN PLUS...

▷ Chesapeake Bay, famous for its crabs and oysters, and close to where the author lives, is the setting for the 1981 Newbery Medal winner **Jacob Have I Loved** (1980). This story, set in the 1940s, is about the hard life of Louise, who works with her fisherman father and resents her twin sister, who seems to have all the talent and privileges. Louise is the elder of the twins, by only a few minutes, but it was her sister Caroline who received all the love and attention. Or so it seemed, until the day Caroline left the island of Rass and Louise slowly began to discover that she too was loved and needed. The title comes from the Bible, 'Jacob have I loved, but Esau have I hated . . .'

▽ Cynthia Voigt was born in Boston, USA, raised in Connecticut and educated at Smith College, Massachusetts where she gained a B.A. degree in English. She worked in a variety of jobs, from secretarial work to waitressing, before becoming a teacher of English at the Key High School in Baltimore. Although this is a demanding full-time job, she somehow manages to combine it successfully with writing. Her husband Walter teaches Latin, Greek and Ancient History at the same school. They have two children, Jessica and Peter. Cynthia Voigt says, 'What is it about teaching that is so interesting? The very things that make writing interesting, I think. Like writing, it keeps the mind alive — I go into a classroom and I am faced with any number of different characters. There are not, I think, many occupations which offer the range of experience that teaching does. Writing happens to be one of them.'

Homecoming (1981), the first of Cynthia Voigt's books about the four abandoned Tillerman children, who decide to make a long and difficult journey overland to find a grandmother they have never met, began with a casual observation and a series of questions: 'About a year before I started to write Homecoming, when I was busy thinking about Tell Me if the Lovers are Losers, I was — as so often I am — in the supermarket parking lot, and I saw — as so often you do — some kids waiting in a station wagon. They weren't waiting in any particular way that I remember, they weren't fighting, they weren't hanging out the windows yelling at passers-by, they weren't weeping miserably. They were just waiting in the car. I don't know why, but I began to wonder: what would happen if the person for whom they were waiting just never came back? And what would happen to the children then?'

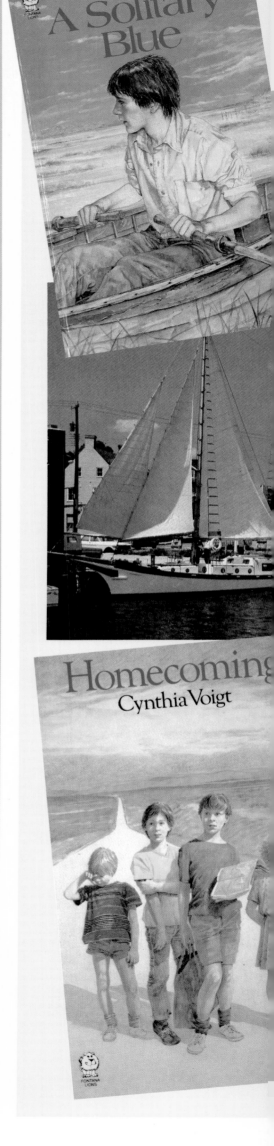

▷ In the sequel to Homecoming, Dicey's Song (1982), Dicey Tillerman (aged 13), her sister Maybeth, and her brothers James and Sammy, move in with their eccentric grandmother. Dicey finds that her troubles are far from over. Dicey's Song won the Newbery Medal for 'the most distinguished contribution to American literature for children'. Cynthia Voigt says that, 'I started writing Dicey's Song in my head even before I finished Homecoming. I had so much of it written in my imagination before I even sat down to actual writing — what had to happen and how the children would react, what problems they would face and what they would find out about themselves, especially Dicey — so much of that was already going on in my mind that I had trouble sitting down to make a plan for the book. It seemed to me that while the adventures were important, more important was how to live an ordinary life, after you had won the prize you wanted.'

◁ In **A Solitary Blue** (1983), Jeff Greene's life is in ruins after his mother walks out on him, leaving him alone with his uncommunicative father. He becomes very withdrawn and unhappy — until he meets Dicey Tillerman, with whom he finds true friendship and warmth. This book, like others in the series, is set in Maryland, on Chesapeake Bay, where Cynthia Voigt lives, in the city of Annapolis. '**A Solitary Blue** was begun before **Dicey's Song** was completed. When I discovered Jeff in **Dicey's Song**, I knew what his story was, and I wanted to write it. These books seem to me — almost — to have been waiting for me to open the door and discover them. They seem that way even though I have notebooks filled with ideas, and plans, and conversations, and lots of questions that read something like, ''How could you get yourself into such a box?'' or ''You don't think you can really do this with them do you?'' '

The Runner (1985), is the story of 'Bullet' Tillerman (Dicey's uncle), the rebellious teenage son of a bullying father. Bullet runs not just to win but for the joy of running. When a new, black runner named Tamer Shipp joins the school team, Bullet agrees to coach him. Tamer and Dicey turn up again in **Come a Stranger**, the story of a girl's thwarted hopes of becoming a ballet dancer. She thinks she has been rejected by her ballet school because she is black, not because she has grown too tall and heavy. Into her life comes Tamer Shipp, who is now a minister of religion, and he helps her over the pain of rejection.

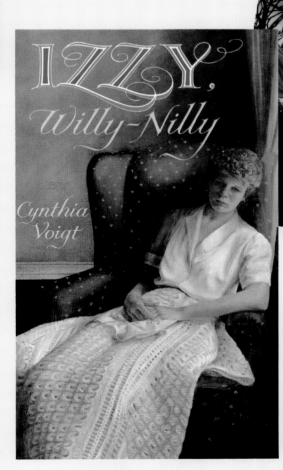

◁ △ Not all of Cynthia Voigt's books are about the Tillerman family. **Jackaroo**, a romance set in the past, has a masked outlaw as its hero. The teenage heroine of **Izzy, Willy-Nilly** has to adjust to life as an amputee, after she is involved in a car accident on her way home from a party. With the help of a friend, Izzy takes her first uncertain steps to a different life. She finds, slowly and painfully, that she is the only one who must redefine who and what she is.

The following are select bibliographies and are meant to be used only as guides. As the 15 diverse and mostly prolific authors represented in this collection have written many books between them, there is not enough space to list every single title they have published. However, in each case, all major works are listed. Inexpensive paperback editions are also indicated, since most of the titles listed have remained in print in this format because of their literary quality and long-lived popularity. US alternatives are listed where UK editions are not available.

Joan Aiken
The Wolves of Willoughby Chase Abelard Schuman/Puffin.
Black Hearts in Battersea Cape/Puffin.
Night Birds on Nantucket Cape/Puffin.
The Whispering Mountain Cape/Puffin.
A Necklace of Raindrops Cape/Puffin.
The Cuckoo Tree Cape/Puffin.
The Kingdom under the Sea Cape/Puffin.
A Harp of Fishbones Cape.
Arabel's Raven BBC.
Midnight Is a Place Cape/Puffin.
Not What You Expected Doubleday.
A Bundle of Nerves Gollancz/Puffin.
Go Saddle the Sea Cape/Puffin.
Tale of a One-Way Street Cape/Puffin.
A Touch of Chill Gollancz.
The Shadow Guests Cape/Puffin.
The Stolen Lake Cape/Puffin.
A Whisper in the Night Gollancz.
Fog Hounds, Wind Cat, Sea Mice Piccolo.

Nina Bawden
Devil by the Sea Collins.
The Secret Passage Gollancz/Puffin.
On the Run Gollancz/Puffin.
The White Horse Gang Gollancz/Puffin.
The Witch's Daughter Gollancz/Puffin.
A Handful of Thieves Gollancz/Puffin.
The Runaway Summer Gollancz/Puffin/M Books.
Squib Gollancz/Puffin.
Carrie's War Gollancz/Puffin.
The Peppermint Pig Gollancz/Puffin.
Rebel on a Rock Gollancz/Puffin.
The Robbers Gollancz/Puffin.
Kept in the Dark Gollancz/Puffin.

Judy Blume
Iggie's House Heinemann/Piccolo.
Are You There, God? It's Me, Margaret Gollancz/Piccolo.
Freckle Juice Heinemann (Banana Books).
Then Again, Maybe I Won't Heinemann/Piccolo.
It's Not the End of the World Heinemann/Piccolo.
Tales of a Fourth Grade Nothing Bodley Head/Piccolo.
Otherwise Known As Sheila the Great Bodley Head/Piccolo.
Deenie Heinemann/Piccolo.
Blubber Heinemann/Piccolo.
Forever Gollancz/Piccolo.
Starring Sally J. Freedman as Herself Bradbury/Piccolo.
Superfudge Bodley Head/Piccolo/M Books.
Tiger Eyes Heinemann/Piccolo.

Lucy M. Boston
The Children of Green Knowe Faber/Puffin.
The Chimneys of Green Knowe Faber/Puffin.
The River at Green Knowe Faber/Puffin.
A Stranger at Green Knowe Faber/Puffin.
An Enemy at Green Knowe Faber/Puffin.
The Stones of Green Knowe Bodley Head/Puffin.
The Castle of Yew Bodley Head.
The Sea Egg Faber/Puffin.
The House That Grew Faber.
Nothing Said Faber.
The Guardians of the House Bodley Head.
The Fossil Snake Bodley Head.

Betsy Byars
The Midnight Fox Faber.
The Summer of the Swans Viking/Hippo.
The House of Wings Bodley Head/Puffin.
The Eighteenth Emergency Bodley Head/Puffin/M Books.
After the Goat Man Bodley Head/Puffin/M Books.
The TV Kid Bodley Head/Puffin/M Books.
The Pinballs Bodley Head/Puffin/M Books.
The Cartoonist Bodley Head/Puffin/M Books.
Good-bye, Chicken Little Bodley Head/Puffin/M Books.
The Night Swimmers Bodley Head/Puffin/M Books.
The Cybil War Bodley Head/Puffin.
The Animal, the Vegetable and John D. Jones Bodley Head/Puffin.
The Two-Thousand Pound Goldfish Bodley Head/Puffin.
The Glory Girl Bodley Head/Puffin.
Cracker Jackson Bodley Head/Puffin.
The Computer Nut Bodley Head/Puffin.

John Christopher
The White Mountains Hamish Hamilton/Puffin.
The City of Gold and Lead Hamish Hamilton/Puffin.
The Pool of Fire Hamish Hamilton/Puffin.
The Lotus Caves Hamish Hamilton/Puffin.
The Guardians Hamish Hamilton/Puffin.
The Prince in Waiting Hamish Hamilton/Puffin.
Beyond the Burning Lands Hamish Hamilton/Puffin.
The Sword of the Spirits Hamish Hamilton/Puffin.
Empty World Hamish Hamilton/Puffin.
Fireball Gollancz/Puffin.
New Found Land Gollancz/Puffin.
Dragon Dance Viking Kestrel/Puffin.

Beverly Cleary
Henry Huggins Morrow/Scholastic.
Ellen Tebbits Morrow.
Henry and Beezus Morrow.
Henry and Ribsy Morrow.
Beezus and Ramona Hamish Hamilton/Puffin.
Fifteen Morrow/Puffin.
Henry and the Clubhouse Hamish Hamilton/Scholastic.
The Mouse and the Motorcycle Hamish Hamilton/Puffin.
Ramona the Pest Hamish Hamilton/Puffin/Junior M Books.
Runaway Ralph Hamish Hamilton/Puffin.
Ramona the Brave Hamish Hamilton/Puffin.
Ramona and Her Father Hamish Hamilton/Puffin.
Ramona and Her Mother Hamish Hamilton/Puffin.
Ramona Forever Hamish Hamilton/Puffin.
Ramona Quimby, Age 8 Hamish Hamilton/Puffin.
Dear Mr Henshaw Julia MacRae/Puffin.

Roald Dahl
James and the Giant Peach Allen & Unwin/Puffin.
Charlie and the Chocolate Factory Allen & Unwin/Puffin.
The Magic Finger Allen & Unwin/Puffin.
Fantastic Mr Fox Allen & Unwin/Puffin.
Charlie and the Great Glass Elevator Allen & Unwin/Puffin.
Danny, the Champion of the World Cape/Puffin.
The Wonderful Story of Henry Sugar Cape/Puffin.
The Enormous Crocodile Cape/Puffin.
The Twits Cape/Puffin.
George's Marvellous Medicine Cape/Puffin.
The BFG Cape/Puffin.
The Witches Cape/Puffin.
Revolting Rhymes Cape/Puffin.
Dirty Beasts Cape/Puffin.
Boy Cape/Puffin.
Going Solo Cape.

Alan Garner
The Weirdstone of Brisingamen Collins.
The Moon of Gomrath Collins.
Elidor Collins/Lions/M Books.
The Owl Service Collins/Lions/M Books.
Red Shift Collins/Lions.
The Stone Book Collins.
Tom Fobble's Day Collins.
Granny Reardun Collins.
The Aimer Gate Collins.
The Guizer Hamish Hamilton.
The Lad of the Gad Collins.

Mollie Hunter
Patrick Kentigern Keenan Blackie.
The Kelpie's Pearls Blackie/Puffin.
A Pistol in Greenyards Evans/Piccolo.
The Ghosts of Glencoe Evans/Piccolo.
The Enchanted Whistle (The Ferlie) Blackie/Magnet.
The Lothian Run Hamish Hamilton/Puffin.
The Thirteenth Member Hamish Hamilton/Puffin.
The Haunted Mountain Hamish Hamilton/Puffin.
A Sound of Chariots Hamish Hamilton/Fontana Lions.
The Stronghold Hamish Hamilton/Piccolo.
A Stranger Came Ashore Hamish Hamilton/Fontana Lions.
The Third Eye Hamish Hamilton.
The Dragonfly Years Hamish Hamilton.

Ursula Le Guin
A Wizard of Earthsea Gollancz/Puffin.
The Tombs of Atuan Gollancz/Puffin.
The Farthest Shore Gollancz/Puffin.
A Very Long Way from Anywhere Else Gollancz/Puffin.
Leese Webster Gollancz.
Threshold Gollancz.

Margaret Mahy
The Dragon of an Ordinary Family Heinemann.
A Lion in the Meadow Dent/Puffin.
The Man Whose Mother Was a Pirate Dent.
The Pirates' Mixed-up Voyage Dent/Magnet.
The Railway Engine and the Hairy Brigands Dent.
The Wind between the Stars Dent.
Leaf Magic Dent/Magnet.
Nonstop Nonsense Dent/Magnet.
The Boy Who Was Followed Home Dent/Magnet.
The Great Piratical Rumbustification and The
   Librarian and the Robbers Dent/Puffin.
The Downhill Crocodile Whizz Dent.
Raging Robots and Unruly Uncles Dent/Puffin.
The Chewing Gum Rescue Dent/Magnet.
The Haunting Dent/Magnet.
The Changeover Dent/Magnet.
The Catalogue of the Universe Dent/Magnet.
The Tricksters Dent/Magnet.
Jam Dent.

Jan Mark
Thunder and Lightnings Kestrel.
Under the Autumn Garden Kestrel/Puffin.
The Ennead Kestrel/Puffin.
Nothing To Be Afraid Of Kestrel/Puffin.
Hairs in the Palm of the Hand Kestrel/Puffin.
The Dead Letter Box Kestrel/Puffin.
Feet and Other Stories Kestrel/Puffin.
Handles Kestrel/Puffin.
Trouble Half-way Kestrel/Puffin.
Out of the Oven Viking/Kestrel.
Frankie's Hat Viking/Kestrel.
At the Sign of the Dog and Rocket Viking/Kestrel.

Katherine Paterson
The Sign of the Chrysanthemum Kestrel.
Of Nightingales That Weep Kestrel.
The Master Puppeteer Crowell.
Bridge to Terabithia Gollancz/Puffin.
The Great Gilly Hopkins Gollancz/Puffin/M
   Books.
Jacob Have I Loved Gollancz/Puffin.
Rebels of the Heavenly Kingdom Gollancz/Puffin.

Cynthia Voigt
Homecoming Collins/Fontana Lions.
Tell Me if the Lovers Are Losers Atheneum.
Dicey's Song Collins/Fontana Lions.
The Callender Papers Atheneum.
A Solitary Blue Collins/Fontana Lions.
Building Blocks Atheneum.
The Runner Collins/Fontana Lions.
Come a Stranger Collins.
Jackaroo Atheneum.
Izzy, Willy-Nilly Atheneum.